salmonpoetry

Publishing Irish & International

Poetry Since 1981

One Small Sun

Paulann Petersen

Published in 2019 by
Salmon Poetry
Cliffs of Moher, County Clare, Ireland
Website: www.salmonpoetry.com
Email: info@salmonpoetry.com

ISBN 978-1-912561-48-3

Cover & Title Page Painting: *"Happy Insomniac Moon" by Josie Gray*
Cover Design & Typesetting: *Siobhán Hutson*

Printed in Ireland by Sprint Print

*Salmon Poetry gratefully acknowledges the support of
The Arts Council / An Chomhairle Ealaíon*

For Ken,
who is my support,
my advocate

Acknowledgments

With gratitude to the editors of the following publications in which these poems first appeared, many in earlier versions:

Asian Reporter: "Lunar New Year"

Atlanta Review: "Fed"

Basalt: "A Proof," "His Place"

Bear Deluxe: "Storytime"

Calyx: "Exposure," "In the Church of the Metamorphosis"

Clackamas Literary Review: "Jotted on the Underside," "When To Say Uncle," "On This Side of the River," "One Chance," "Offerings," "Half the Telling"

Clover: "Fractional," "My Map of the 1950's," "At the Foster Home," "Come So Low"

High Desert Journal: "Protest," "Passage"

Home Address: "Home Address"

Hubbub: "Divine Intervention"

Portland Lights: "Belated"

North Dakota Review: "Your Glass Face in the Rain"

Notre Dame Review: "Semblance," "Nested"

Oregon English Journal: "Even Then, I Must Have Known," "Elegy, 1980"

Prairie Schooner: "With Christmas Season Hard Upon Us"

Timberline Review: "Grace," "Nonesuch," "The Turnover," "Vocation"

Weber Studies: "Admission"

With gratitude to the members of Poetry Church, Pearls, and Odds for commenting on many of these individual poems; to Greg Simon for reading the manuscript in an earlier form; to Andrea Hollander, whose astute counsel was invaluable in bringing *One Small Sun* into its present form.

Contents

iii. SMALL SUNS

i. Anthems

EVEN THEN, I MUST HAVE KNOWN

—for my father Paul Whitman, 1912-1988

"Better come over, P.A.," you'd said
on the phone, "You've got to see,
the poor old guy wrote on walls," and I'd
resisted, my day so wed to must-do's
that even with you stopped
dead in your tracks waiting,
I'd wanted to refuse.
             "Don't dilly-dally now,
I'm not pulling another nail until you get here,"
was the prod to make me set aside
what I was doing and drive over,
some part of me turning the steering wheel
left then right, pressing down
on the gas and brakes as my mind sorted
and unsorted what I'd left behind,
undone.
          "Over here, P.A.," you called
as I walked from the car, "You'll be glad
you came"—you motioning to that maze
of lean-to's you were razing, chain
of jerry-built breezeways and sheds
spreading back from the old bachelor's
one-room house facing us.
            Couldn't I tell
as I read it, the first of those messages
you'd called me to see, missives made
by an old man who'd lived alone
for over thirty years, his words chalked
in a careful hand on bare planks?
"Didn't I say they were something, P.A.?"
You smiling then, "There, right
over there," pointing to more
above a low baffle.

Couldn't I see?
In time—not having written them down—
I'd fail to remember those words
so singular they'd require me
to later reinvent them. Surely without
that dead man's irretrievable words,
with you, Father, no longer alive,
not here to ask, I'll never get it
right. I'll be left with
making it up.
                    "Well, was it worth it?
Did I figure right?" You stand there,
leaning on your rake—your pry bar,
your hammer against a stack
of tarpaper and wood debris
where you propped them,
stopping to wait
for me.
            You reach into a back pocket
for a blue-edged handkerchief,
"OK, Baby, it's back to work now.
Give me a hug before you go."
You wipe dust off
the frameless glasses
you've taken from that face
I've no need to reinvent,
one I know by heart—
you now knowing I've seen
what you called me
                        to see.

MAGNOLIAS

—for my mother Grace Whitman, 1914-1995

Black faille suits skimmed
at the waist, hats with a corolla of veil,
gloves, pumps. Daubs of the Tabu
they shared—one behind an earlobe,
one at that wrist-spot where Mom's fingers
had learned to count a pulse, one onto
a nylon stocking's black seam,
to scent the soft strip of skin
behind a knee.
                        Mom and Rena
dressed up *fit to kill*. Mom near the end
of nurse's training at St. Mary's—
single and rooming with Rena
and her husband Merle
in their cottage under a huge
magnolia's shade. Early dusk,
early winter fog, Rena and Mom
Skylarking, on a cable car
headed to San Francisco's swank
Mark Hopkins Hotel.
                        Just in time to catch
the cocktail crowd, Gimlets
in the top-floor lounge where men
hovered around them, a hand sliding
along the marble bar to nudge—
toward the barkeep—money
to cover their drinks.
                        Tiger-eye cufflinks
winked from the swell's dress shirt,
him murmuring "My pleasure."
"Stardust," "It's Only a Paper Moon"
adrift from the piano. A second round,
"My treat, this time," coming from
another swell.

Grabbing their purses—
black clutch bags—they were off
to the powder room. To pee.
To wash their hands with musk-blossoms
of milled soap. To press new curves
of red into their lips, pale powder
onto their already
milky skin.   Leaving the Ladies' Room,
they skirted the bar. Unnoticed.
They sidled out of the lounge, riding
the elevator's long outtake of breath
down to the lobby. A second or two
to nudge elbows, to half swallow a laugh.
They headed back.   In Rena's front yard
a bud had opened. The tree kept up
a year-round gala of broad gleaming leaves,
a few tight folds of cream swelling
even in December. Hands-down gorgeous.
Huge candlewax blooms steeped
in lemony perfume.
                    Top of the Mark.
A little harmless fun. Before anything
had a chance to get out of hand,
Mom and Rena, gone.
Petals fell on the clipped lawn,
a scatter of crescent moons—
their edges
                    dark in winter sun.

FRACTIONAL

"I love my daughter, but I wish
God had given me ten sons."

—my mother's mother

My mother being worth a fraction
of my uncle, it would have taken
many of her to equal him. Five plus five
registered nurses who made highest
scores on their state boards. Five times two
trained assistants who helped pioneer
open-heart surgery. Even then, she would be
only even with her brother.
                              Ten daughters
who could devote themselves
that much more to my grandmother—
more of them to cringe at Nana's anger,
to yearn to inherit at least a tiny
portion of her panache.
                              Ten wives
to take care to earn a fraction
less than my breadwinner father
made each year. As many mothers to insist
on working the day shift to be free evenings
to drive me to dancing lessons
at the House of Leon—watching
my stuttered attempts at foxtrot, waltz, samba
made to a record player's blare of songs
in four-four, three-four,
two-four times.

At least ten sisters-in-law
to my uncle's one wolf-whistle wife.
Her D-cup breasts held
their cleavaged sway above the nip
of a waist encircled by a belt cinched in
to the last eyelet—drawing
compliments toward her trim midriff.
Pancake make-up. Rouge. Mascara.
Penciled eyebrow arches.
                              Thick-torsoed,
heavy-ankled, my mother used
only lipstick. Only that and a cologne
called Emeraude, its green package on sale
at our corner drugstore. Its name was French
for a gem precious and brilliant enough
to eclipse even envy's sting.
                              If I were now
to catch the slightest
trace of that scent, I could
breathe my dear mother in. Alive, again.
That's all it would take.
Just one tenth of
                    a tenth's drop.

JOTTED ON THE UNDERSIDE

—for my grandmother, Ann Theobald

Sixteen words, that's all.
One misspelled, two capitalized
for emphasis, two others
each solo on a line.
                              In your cursive,
they scrawl across the back
of a black and white Brownie snapshot
taken of you and Nell posed outside,
in your garden.
                              A sentence to tell
what Nell said. A fragment to explain
what she meant. An enquiry lacking
a question mark.
                              You and your best friend
stand in 40's dresses—black, tailored,
blunt-shouldered. Both of you wear
a hat listing sharp to the right—
left eyes struck by sunshine, rights
swooped into shadow. Rakish,
folks said of you two.
Nell's hat, a dark straw skimmer.
Yours, an even darker pillbox
that sprouts, at your forehead,
a pale silk blossom
big as your fair-skinned face
lifting to the camera.
                              You both wear
white gloves, of course. It's summer.
You and Nell dressed to the nines.
Your backs are turned to the street,
the camera held low to get
a full-length view, to catch—

in the foreground—your garden's
pride, tall white lilies, each stalk
bugling a fanfare of blooms.
You're long dead. Nell too.
Still, I talk to you, Nana,
there in your side yard
standing next to a flower bed
no one has tended in decades.
You answer me, saying
the sixteen words
lying beneath your likeness
alive in that garden.

Nell says Here
are the Prettiest
flowers in the
yard. Meaning
us.
Aren't the Lillies
grand.

Before you fall
silent, you pose your final question—
so sure in your asking,
you choose a mark
to make of it
an anthem.

RITUAL

—for my grandfather, Archie Theobald (1890 -1955)

Sundays, you didn't work, your fur shop
silent. In its front window, the CLOSED sign
turned itself neatly toward the traffic
on Sandy Boulevard. Any Sunday,
I might have been staying with you and Nana,
there for the weekend. Every Sunday, the Oregonian
arrived on your front porch, thick and weighted
with the ink of extra ads. Sunday's comics
were printed in color—Slugo and Sparkle Plenty
wearing deep, bright hues.
                   We looked at the paper—
you, the front section—me, Parade and the comics—
and when we were done, I carried
its bulk away. In a stack by the back porch door,
I found Saturday's paper, skimpy and by then
in slip-shod folds, curling at its edges. I turned
to its comic strip page and smoothed it out
on the chrome-edged kitchen table. I fetched
your box of colored pencils, a whole Faber set
with every basic color—as well as
the rare ones in between.
                  In black and white,
Saturday's comics were starkly drawn,
each character and object outlined
in ink, those wan spaces in every panel
waiting for us resident artists. Little Orphan Annie
got her red hair. Dick Tracy's suit shouldered
its detective blue. Trees leafed out. Skies cleared.
In Prince Valiant's crown the jewels
grew precious. Veronica put on lipstick.
Blondie bespoke her name.

Now that I've lived
for years beyond the age at which you died,
I see—more clearly than ever—those Sundays.
You sit at the kitchen table, me at your side,
our heads together, bowed to our work.
Your slacks are charcoal, your shirt beige.
The metal parts of your wheelchair, silver.
In your fingers a cigar gleams
its bronzed brown, the lit end flaring
into ember-red each time you take a puff.
As you exhale, your breath becomes
the color of smoke. In slow swirls,
it eases upward, meanders the air,
leaving its trace below—
that ghost
            of steel-gray ash.

WHAT TRAVELLED HIS BODY

A wide pine plank
in a furrier's work room.
One of several boards
he uses to stretch and shape
animal skins. Wheelchair-bound,
he calls on his shoulders and arms
to funnel strength into his hands
as he works, nailing a wet pelt
to the wood's surface. This furrier is
my grandfather. The board's edge
is rough, untamed. His right forearm
jams against that edge as he strains
to keep the board steady. A coarse sliver
drives into his arm. Deep.
Swift sharp pain. A bubble of blood.
Then welcome numbness. Tomorrow comes,
and his arm doesn't hurt. He ignores
the long, thick intruder. Out of sight,
never to mind, and onward into the ongoing
business of animal skins passing through
his hands—stacks to be matched, let out,
whip-stitched, trimmed.
                              Each weekday
in the fur shop he wheels
from table to table to work the pelts,
his palms blackened by the rubber tires.
At home, Nana must help him
onto and off the toilet, into and out
of bed. Once she's helped lower him
into the bathtub, she rubs the wet washcloth
with a block of soap, lathering
his shoulders and back. This winter day,
the air is cold, the bathwater hot.

Steam carries the soap's musk
into their breath. A sudsy film eases
her hand across his back to a spot
above his left shoulder blade,
her fingers meeting with a hardness.
A pointed bump. She peers.
She presses. A long, thick
wood sliver slips out.

                            A scrap of forest,
the splinter of pine has journeyed
his body for months—
up his arm, along his shoulder,
across his back. Body-traveler,
this remnant dwelled within him, delving
into his flesh to roam.

                              The animals
dwell there, too. Mink, fox, fitch,
sable, marten—all bits
of a feral world that lodges
inside him. From the dappled
forest of their home, they come
into the darkness of his hands
working their skins.
Then emerge, once more.
The stoles, the muffs, the coats,
they gleam—giving off
the weight of their
                        wild light.

THROUGH THAT WINDOW
I CALL MY OWN

—Portland, Oregon, 1949

i.

From the cab of his black truck,
the vegetable man cries out
as he drives down my Nana's street.
A Chinaman. I've never seen
a truck like his before, so old-fashioned
and high, open on the sides and back.
All his produce overflows the crates,
green and yellow and red, bouncing
and flopping as he drives along.
He sings "CARROTS CABBAGE KALE,"
the sounds inside each vegetable name
so strange, I couldn't make out
his words at all, if I didn't already know
who he is.
                    My Nana doesn't buy
from him. She does take her scissors
to that regular man who pedals by
on a cart that carries his big grindstone.
On the sidewalk, I stand close to watch him
turn the sandpapery wheel. Faster and faster,
until he touches the scissor blade to its gray blur
and the thousand tiny sparks begin to fly
like a Fourth of July sparkler.
                              I run to the street
when the scissor-sharpener comes by.
But when the Chinaman comes, I stay
inside, looking out at him through
one of the little square window panes
rising in two high stacks to either side
of Nana's front door—that window
just the height of my eyes.

                                    He's small,
not a lot taller than me. His hair's longer
than mine, its water-wet shine woven
into a braid. He wears a black blouse
fastened by cloth knots my Nana says
are *frogs*. No buttons, no snaps, just *frogs*.
Animals keep his blouse from flying open.
He has a tiny cap, pants loose and soft,
shoes made from cloth. All in black.
His skin glows tight across his face,
like the yellow plums Nana buys at Keinow's.
That same plum-light shines from inside
his face. People say a Chinaman has
slant eyes, but his eyes are deep-dark,
they're narrow, they crinkle at their
outside corners, like gathered silk.

He's beautiful.
                    Entirely.

        ii.

I believe he knows how to slip
a fat golden ring over a bird's head
and down its neck so it can't swallow
the fish it catches, fish it will give
to him—just like the fisherman from China
in a story I read at school. I believe such a bird,
black as his own hair, lays its head
and curved neck onto his outstretched hands,
giving him the sequined fish it's caught,
one by one.
                    At night the two go inside
their floating house called a *junk*. But it's not
junky at all. It has chairs and a sofa covered
in velvet dark as an eggplant's skin.
The kitchen is full of pots and pans

24

made from real silver. The Chinaman slips
the ring off the bird's neck, hanging it
from an ivory hook on the wall. He says,
"Go now, Shiny One. Fly out into the night
as black as you. Dive into the river as dark
and gleaming as your feathers. Catch
fish after fish after fish. Swallow them whole.
Come back when your belly is round and full.
While you're gone, I will cook
what you held for me safe in your throat.
Go. I will leave a lamp burning for you
in the window. Mine will be
the face you can see behind
the lighted square of glass
when you come home."

He calls these words
to the bird as it flies out and over the water
dotted with stars. Then he's quiet,
his black braid swooping forward
when he leans over his pan to cook
a silver-sided fish.

The whole world
grows silent then.

So silent, I'm afraid
if ever this Chinaman spoke to me,
my tongue would knot, my throat close.
I'd have no voice, nothing
to say. To a man like him,
nothing beautiful

enough to say.

TADPOLE

Tiny dark squirmer, your tail
flicks and twists to zip you along.
Water-bound now, you will grow up,
your body opening to swallow
that tail. Your gills will shape themselves
into air-craver lungs. Flank-buds
will sprout into arms and legs.
Once you're a frog, you will drink
rain through your skin.
                              You are first fish,
then animal, then dead in the winter
before you rouse to make
your shameless croaks in spring—
splaying your hind legs in a way
so that any woman can see how to open
hers to give birth.
                         But now you are
this fat-bodied fishlet, and I
a small girl, walking the five blocks
from the Presbyterian Church to home.
An hour ago at day camp,
on a creek's bank, we were each given
a Dixie cup to scoop
some of you up, to take you away.
The only one I caught, you swim
in my paper cup's bit of water.
After holding you steady on the bus ride
from camp to church, I step
slowly, slowly, watching for the juts
where tree roots lift the concrete,
ready to stumble me.

                              A crow calls.
I look up. If I could, I would watch
this sound squirting its dark arrow
from the crow's throat into my ears.
But all I see are black eyes,
looking at me. I look down.
                                     Near the toe
of my scuffed shoe, the sidewalk
has grown a shallow puddle no wider
than my fist. While I didn't watch,
my hand let the Dixie cup
tilt. Now that puddle
is gone, swallowed down
into the concrete. Amid its darkness
you are a black dot.
Unmoving.
                        I will grow up to kiss
the Prince's nubbled, wet lips.
I will spread my legs. Inside me,
he will set loose his fierce
whip-tailed swimmers, the half
of me that's missing. Waters within me
will break, gush, fall—
at my feet, a wet
                        indelible stain.

TELLING

Alive in our room
at Richmond Grade School,
the new girl was so much unlike
our Dick and Jane, bright red ball,
green grass, Look! See!
reading-primer-lives,
she might have emerged
from some farthest place
of the world, except she didn't.
Yet did, because I was sure
I'd seen her first on the pages
of a book.
                    She'd taken her face
from a Dust Bowl story,
one I'd just read all on my own
in Miss Bertha Harrison's second grade class.
Her sharp-line features matched
her strings of arms and legs sticking out
from the faded plaid of her cotton wash-dress.
She was a come-to-life twin of that drawn girl
in a story about deep dust, loose
and blowing.
                    Living on land flattened
by washed-out color, that storygirl walked
a thin dirt road, dust rising in curling puffs
wherever she took a step. On both sides
of the road were rows of corn gone gray.
Crops so withered her family would—
by the last pages—load
its quilts and chair and crib
onto a truck and move west across
the westward turning pages

of a picture book in our Portland
ever so green Oregon
schoolroom.
                    Skinny in a way that I—
thin as I was—would never be,
quiet in a way my wisps of shyness
could scarcely recognize, the new girl came
and went for two weeks. Then didn't.
"Baby sister, a newborn," Miss Harrison said,
and the girl's absence for that past week
was something I could *maybe*
understand. Some family strangeness
had wrapped around her house so tight
she couldn't put on that one dress she wore,
slip the strands of her brown hair
into their braids, slip herself
out the door and off to school
in those days after her baby sister
had arrived.

        ii.

Show and Tell were words
I waited for each week, a chance to bring
a birthday toy. Like my walking-doll
Elizabeth Ann. With feet big enough
to need a real baby's shoes. Or something
even stranger like the box of baby pigs
my mother borrowed for a day
through a fellow nurse
who knew a farmer. "Piglet! Piglet!"
we cried, as we each got a turn
holding one tiny mass of twisting
soft-skinned pink over the box
in case we faltered and dropped
that squealing baby.

                    "At home," said the new girl
now back at school and standing in front
of our lined-up wooden desks,
"My sister was born
at home." And I could bring to mind
only the rows of fat pink faces
above their pastel cones of wrapped blanket
at the hospital where my mother worked.
"Born at our house," she said.
                                        Her turn to tell
for Show and Tell, and some
separate world holding her was spinning
away from the known world
where my feet stood.
"I delivered Mama's baby.
By myself. At home."
                                Then silence.
Not a single let-loose sound.
Then Miss Harrison's stop
to Show and Tell, the "Everybody
at your desks, go on, hurry now."
Her hand on the new girl's jut of shoulder,
nudging her along. "Let's open our books
to today's story," while color's heat
rose in my babied cheeks.
While the dustbowl face
of that story girl
showed not even
                    a mote of red.

WHY I DIDN'T PUT OUT

Three girls. One for each bedroom
upstairs at Nana's. One each
for her living room's trio of easy chairs.
They sat, prim and showered.
Pedal-pushers, blouses, ironed.
Sleeveless blouses that flared into crisp
cotton tents—the better not to cling
to the curve of their hard, risen
bellies. Unwed mothers-to-be.
Girls rooming and boarding
at my grandmother's house. A place—
far enough from their hometowns—
to stay unknown until
they delivered.
                    In this house of a widow
in need of extra income, each had
her own room. Each her spot at Nana's
dining room table. Each must have been
bored—counting the days of a second
or third trimester.
                    Ann's granddaughter
was coming to visit. I could imagine Nana
telling them, "I want you to meet her.
Get cleaned up. Come downstairs.
She'll be here sometime
after three."
                    In the front room of a home
for the unwed and expecting, I sat
facing them. We talked. A granddaughter
on a visit, I was a girl
close enough in age to be
one of them. I think I spoke kindly.
I'm certain I knew in any world
other than *that* one, we four

could have been friends. But I know
without a doubt I then had
little sense—other than shame—
of what must have been filling
their thoughts to the point their minds
swelled shut.
                    Him. The baby's father.
That shuddered release from his
hard-pumping dick. The broken rubber.
The distant sound of his phone
ringing, ringing, ringing
unanswered, each time she called.
The look on the face of her own mother,
when the girl finally—she was already
showing—had to confess.
                              The baby.
Everyone said it would grow to seem
huge inside her, but tiny once
she'd pushed it out.
She'd hold that baby maybe
once, before giving it up
to the nurse who would
give it over into some waiting
couple's arms. People
she'd never see.
                    After her hospital stay,
I knew each girl would be back at Nana's
for a while. Long enough to bind
her breasts into submission.
Enough days for her milk to stop
leaking through the thickly-wound cloth.
Time enough to have stopped
crying enough to ride the bus
those hours needed to reach
home again.
                    Those three, surely they
hated me. They had to have known

how much I didn't want to ever be
who they'd suddenly become.
In that front room of the far-away house
where they'd been sent to hide
and wait, how could anything less than
hatred suffice for the one who sat,
facing them?
                    I didn't forget those girls.
Soon enough, I loved his fingers—
whichever boyfriend he was—slicking
that dark parting between my thighs.
But I went only so far. I knew
just enough to know I wanted
never to have to come face to face
with someone I could only
come to hate.
                    Least of all, me.

MY MAP OF THE 1950s

On the route I walked to and from
Richmond Grade School,
a huge chestnut tree—
its white flowers each blotched
by a pinprick of red—
bloomed and then burdened
a gutter with the sexual weight
of its burrs. First grade to eighth—
through the blur of my spurting growth—
I stared. Each pod had prickly lips
that parted to expose a dark
glisten-slick seed.
               Halfway down a hallway
embedded with high school lockers,
my barely-remembered combination
opened a metal door clanging
in gray echoes. The boy taller
than any man in my family
appeared there each morning—
his long black fingers
handing me the sentence or two
he'd penciled onto a piece
of lined notebook paper—
some postscript to his secret phone call
of the night before.
              There was the expressway
of his phone number to mine. A route
his voice took each school night to find me
alone, doing homework—reading
a time-rubbed tragedy, or a chapter
from *America for Us All* outlining
cause and effect of our nation's
Civil and uncivil wars. What I set
aside to hear the sinuous inroads
of his voice.

The path my eyes took
up the lean length of his body,
there was always that waywardness.
The legs I'd seen unclothed
on basketball courts. The sinewed
torso.
His deep-of-night eyes
keeping track, following
mine.
        After high school, there were
the decades of us living
both cities and worlds
apart. Then suddenly not.
The secret phone calls
of our midlife. Him married.
Me not. The ring I answered
at 2 A.M., 3, or 4. The narcotic
musk of his voice. A few
brief meetings. A single kiss,
its salt-sweet taste
lingering on my lips until
I licked it too quickly away.
Those years when he had
my number, when I never
knew his. The uncharted silence
ensuing once I, at last, said
No more.
        I no more know how
to decipher that black and white
terrain of my young life
than I did then. But I watch its map
flood—again and again—
with my longing's indelible hues.
Hand-colored, by memory.
In shades bright
as the blood staining
a chestnut's
        milky bloom.

TRESPASS

—*for Geneva Jones*

He's nudging me into your kitchen—
the smoke-musk of his skin, his lank
and length behind me so near I can feel
his heat. Your favorite son lets you know
I'm here. As quickly as you turn your eyes
toward me, a strange caustic air has reached me
even sooner. Its rasp stings my breath.
Tears blur my eyes.
                              Onto your daughter's hair
you're slathering something so acrid my voice
snags in my throat before I can finish saying
"Hello, Mrs. Jones."
                              Conk.
Years will have to pass before I'll know
that word. Right now, I can only guess
this smell must belong to some unthinkably
potent home perm—unlike the Toni kits
on the corner drug store's center aisle,
the ones my friends use to curl
their limp-straight hair.
                              A conk job.
I smell—for a first time—
the singe of self-disdain
without knowing its name.
I've stepped into your kitchen.
Unwelcome. I know this as well
as I know my own name. And I don't.
I cannot know—not yet—that name
you know to be mine.
                              Miss Ann.
A Black name for the white woman.
I'm the *Miss Ann* your favored son

favors, the girl you want to go away,
to leave your son be. I'm the one
he's brought home, into your kitchen—
while you're doing what's a mystery to me,
straightening his sister's hair,
searing her hair so it will wave
and sweep, turning itself into a smooth
pert flip. So her hair will look
more like mine.
                    Raising your head
from your task, you lift
a fierce scant-smile toward me.
You nod at me, saying the name
my mother gave me.
                    I get it,
even though I don't. I know only
that I don't belong.
                    You needn't fear.
I lack—and will not find—the courage
to make my way into this *here* of where
I now am. Although one day, I will at least
begin to understand. It will be decades
before the *Miss Ann* of who I am
stands guard
over a favorite
                    son of her own.

SMITTEN

*—a high school girls' club holds a rummage sale
to raise funds in Portland, 1957*

They won't wait,
don't want to give us the chance
to get our coats off, our wet umbrellas stashed,
the cash box out and ready.
The rummage lady shoos them
back outside. I want them in.
And soon the gypsies are inside,
these women and girls who wear
bouquets of long, gathered skirts
as if they were hostesses at a huge party
in this rummage-room of a home.
On their blouses, stitched-silk flowers
flourish across their bodices, down their sleeves,
along their cuffs. A chevroned sash circles
one gypsy's waist. Another has knotted
a red scarf to make herself a cap—
black curls bursting from under its edges.
Another wears a vest of purple velvet
quilted with shining scarlet thread.
Bangles from wrist to forearm. Earrings so long
they brush a shoulder.
                              The lady
running the rummage room
knew. Get here early, she said,
the gypsies will be waiting at the door.
She opened that door to us
yesterday morning, stood aside
as we carried in the cardboard boxes
full of donated cast-offs. There, the lady said,
put all your kitchen stuff
on that big table in the center.

All the shoes and purses on the table
toward the back. The real junk
on that table nearest the door.
The clothes go on these wire hangers—
put them on the racks
along the wall.
                    Everything had to be
out of the boxes so once we'd gone home,
the rummage lady could lock
the doors tight and set off the billow
of chemical smoke that would
fumigate all through the night.
                              Quick,
these gypsy women flip
through the long rack of clothes,
their fingers tingling for a bit
of slubbed silk, taffeta moiré,
the animal-pelt of velvet's shorn surface.
All the smart, sensible
navy and black, tweed and worsted,
they ignore. Embroidery. Beading.
Finely fastened sequins. Braid. Fringe.
A blouse with convex buttons
crusted in rhinestones.
                        They pay.
One girl reaches into
a drawstring purse made from brocade.
Another into a deep pocket
at the side-seam of her rustling skirt.
A woman reaches under her blouse,
dipping into her cleavage, her fingers
emerging with silvery
quarters and dimes.
                    They're gone.
Out into the steely, wet
Portland morning. Out onto
this downtown street, the dull

bleak of stone and concrete.
Here, fumigant commands the air
with an acrid weight. Looking out
from a window hazed with grime,
I watch a bright stream
of skirts crossing the street.
A wisp of gypsy perfume
deepens
          my breath with its musk.

HAND-ME-DOWN

—five black and white snapshots
  of my grandmother Ann

                i.

From this unpainted farmhouse set on the edge
of a northern lake—Halls Lake whose shoreline grays
with grasses, hazes with the fevers of gangly growth—
my grandmother wanders her childhood.
A girl of seven, arms folded across
her one cotton wash dress, eyes narrowed
at hard sun. *Johnnie*, others call her, short for
Ann Johnson from Minden, Ontario, Canada.
One day she'll be called
                        Canuck.

                ii.

Here she's standing at the steps to a flat
in San Francisco, as far from the farm
as marriage and new clothes can reach.
Cloche hat pulled over one eye, Ann Theobald,
nee Johnson, hems her chemise high
above her knees, rolls her silk stockings
down. Between her skirt and the sheen
of hose
        a shock of white thigh gleams.

                iii.

Annie poses at home in Portland—
daughter, husband, and herself all costumed
for Halloween. Archie, a furrier, dresses
as a caveman, a huge leopardskin

wrapping his body, the pelt's furless edges
a soft ripple down one arm. Burlap wound
over his shoes, a foxtail around his head,
he's smudged his own skin dark. His pupils
stare out from the white of his eyes
like an animal's protective spots.
Annie's done herself up as the devil
in a satin jumpsuit clinging to her stomach,
her breasts. Its tight hood sprouts
long satin horns. From between her legs
a tail curls.

    Just thirteen, Grace is the child-bride
in a long dress with row after row of ruching,
organdy flowers ribboned to her head.
A tasseled prayerbook held between her hands,
my mother-to-be is the white centerpiece
of these three, each looking toward the lens.
Annie's the only one grinning,
a single lock of hair escaping
her devil's cap. Arm extended in front
of my mom, she plants a cardboard trident—
her pitchfork—against
that pale
    backdrop of bridal gown.

iv.

A young grandmother outside her house,
here is that devil and her best friend Nell.
In wide-lapelled, nip-waisted suits,
their eyes flash *to the nines*
under the tilted angle of fancy hats.
Mrs. Arthur Theobald, Annie, now Nana,
stands behind her bed of lilies blooming
like a sweep of white birds veered into flight.
My Archie, the furrier, is inside,

not in sight—confined now
to a wheelchair.
                        He dresses each day
in a three-piece suit, a flower in the buttonhole
of his lapel. Bachelor's Button, Cosmos,
a rose when they're in bloom. Boutonniere.
At Nana's bidding, I run outside to find
the right rosebud, barely unfurled. He sits
in his wheelchair, smiling at me.
On Archie's lapel I pin what grows
from my grandmother's
                        pebbly garden.

        v.

At Cannon Beach, waves roil over us—
Annie and me, me and my Nana—squatting
in shallow surf where white foam can catch us,
douse us into more screams and laughter.
Arms wrapped tight around each other, we look
straight at the camera, mouths stretched in joy—
her blouse and hair sprayed with saltwater,
her sopping pedal-pushers rolled up
her thighs. She takes me with her everywhere—
to the fur shop, to Keinow's Market, away
to this beach. They say I'm her perfect,
her pet. On the drive home, we spot
apples. She pulls the car off the road,
parks it under high branches growing over
a farmer's orchard fence. Nana climbs
onto the top of her sedan, stands on its roof
to pick. What's gleaming,
what's red, she hands
                        down to me.

WHEN TO SAY UNCLE

—for Richard Theobald, my mother's brother

Tell me about the war.
Not mortuary school before
you enlisted, not opening that key
vein in the neck, blood running out
easy, fast into a stainless steel pan.
Enough about the makeup
to make a wife sigh, *Nice,*
he looks peaceful, like he's only
asleep. An illusion to fool grief.
Not that. No tricks. For now,
put your white hankie back
into your pocket.
                    Tell about being
an Army medic, with Nana at home
stateside, content, believing that you—
her only son—wouldn't be sent
to the front lines.
                    But you were.
Tell how—sent in first
to bring supplies—you ducked
behind the crates while a shimmy
from Japanese machine guns
shredded bundles of bandages.
Your life saved by a materiel
of mercy.
                    Home from the war,
handkerchief out, you'd make a knot,
another knot, a twist, and a white
mouse ran up and down your arm.
I shrieked, laughed, watching
its cotton ears twitch
and wave.

Tatters of gauze
must have littered New Guinea mud
around those shot-up crates that day.
How many buddies did you later
bandage, wrapping white around
a limb, pressing soft squares
onto a groaning chest?
How much red throbbed out—
fast, easy—before you could?
Bandages are always white.
For a while. Did those GIs
look peaceful once
they died?
                    I never got to see
the professional tricks you bought
and learned, secrets only
real magicians knew—
just the hankie-mouse, a stunt
to entertain kids. Each time
I saw you, I begged for it.
After the war, you abandoned
being a mortician. *Too much
death*, you said. *Enough
is enough.*
                    Once you were making
your living calling on physicians—
leaving your salesman's trail
of patter and jokes along with samples
of your company's miracle drugs—
did you charm those doctors
into prescribing your brand?
Could you convince them
to scrawl its trade name
onto a white paper square—
their writing a life-saving
sleight of hand?
                    The flags for truce

45

are always white. Only it will do
for such waving. Tell me about
the wages of war. Could enough
ever be enough? Talk about
the bales of gauze, bullet-cut
into bits. Torn, adrift. Tell me
you recall South Pacific wind
scattering those suddenly
useless bandages, countless shreds
blown along a jeep-rutted road—
all those tiny
                    white flags, waving.

PROTEST

—Klamath Falls, March 5, 1983,
  for my son Chris

The State Patrol freezes traffic
just after a school bus squeezes through,
you waving from its yellow cocoon,
bound for a nearby town to play your violin,
me waving back from the highway's shoulder.
I stand among the families and a scatter
of union members waiting with protest signs.
BUY BOOKS NOT BOMBS.
EMPLOYMENT NOT DEPLOYMENT.
NO NEW JOBS IN EL SALVADOR.
The rest of the President's scheduled route
is a daisy chain of best-wishers.
WE LOVE YOU, RONNIE!
KEEP AMERICA STRONG!
THANK YOU FOR THE YEAR
OF THE BIBLE! Mile after mile,
they wait for him
to pass by.
                    At home tonight we'll watch
the news on local TV—Reagan's black limo
speeding into view, its tires throwing out
a screen of winter road-dirt
as we raise our signs with a shout.
You'll yell, "Mom, I can see you. Hey!
There you are!" You'll tell me again
that the average age of a soldier
in Vietnam was nineteen. "War
of the young and the poor," you say.
You're fourteen.
                    In our high school lobby,
each weekday, a recruiter sits. Polished,

groomed. Local boy sent home by the Army,
ready to tell how he's made good.
Career advisor, travel agent, he hands out
presents. Army calendars. Ball point pens.
Book protectors to conceal—
in camo blotches of khaki and green—
Our Living World and *America for Us All.*
The recruiter's table faces our school mascot.
Ten foot Viking. Helmet, spear, shield.
Gift to our school—a chainsaw sculpture
made by metal teeth spun into
an old-growth fir.
                    Now a black copter
hovers over our President's route.
It tilts and dips, its blades a blur
of rapid chops. Kingsley Airbase jets
peel off strips of the sky. A suited man
with dark glasses and walkie-talkie
materializes, inches from my side.
A cop steps out in front of us, gives
final instructions: "Please understand.
From now on *no one* steps on the pavement.
Don't anyone make a move for the road.
If you drop something, don't go after it.
And whatever you do,
hold on
          tight to your kids."

EXPOSURE

—for my daughter Edie

Thirteen, you headed for overgrown shrubs
like a dowser bent on artesian bliss,
your divining rod of shears leaving
a green mound below each bare branch.
I lectured on happy mediums. Your stepdad
winced, then laughed. But you, a girl
with one foot in each camp—
this house/your father's house, each your
half-way house—just shrugged.
It'll never show
by summer, you said.
                       At sixteen,
it was our dog's plumed tail,
your scissor blade against the skin to get
all the burrs. While the dog slapped
its warm rope on my legs, I squirmed
and wished for partial measures I knew
would never work.
                      Then nineteen.
You shaved your head. Bared each bump,
each hollow of your skull. Home to visit
from your father's house, you sometimes
wore a beret but mostly chose
to expose a freshly-peeled self.
You got an old 8 X 10 of your dad
as a crew-cut teen and held it—
a smiling twin—next to your face.
Entirely his. A proud Athena sprung
from your father's young self.
But while I flinched at the quick
you made me see, while I grieved for us
torn apart, you said, "Mom, take a look.
It's already
                growing back."

NESTED

—*for Maya Arun Adarkar, who became my daughter-in-law*

From a Bombay store to this New England flat
you've brought a set of gleaming dubbas,
nest of stainless steel canisters each opening
to reveal a smaller self—each now lying
separate, big to small along a pantry shelf,
containers for pasta, for sugar and flour,
their pale drifts.
                          In the bedroom you share
with my son, you keep an old dubba,
width of a thumbprint, worn to silver
by years of touch. Your mother's
Udi Dubba, vessel of sacred ash,
gift she carried—when she was your age—
from the saintly Sai Baba's fire.
                                    Painted roses
flare their red on the nest of wooden dolls
I give you this Christmas day.
They bloom across the belly
of the largest, a stout Saint Nikolas.
Inside him are two, three and four,
and five peasant girls smaller
and smaller, the last no bigger than
a little finger's final joint. Opening this gift—
what is meant to be opened—you break it
apart to find the girl made
whole again.
                          Onto your finger's tip
you press a shadow
of the Udi Dubba's silver ash,
then touch its blessing to my forehead,
to the nest of dolls, to each gift
this holiday brings—ash

from your mother's talisman,
a vessel of memory small enough
to carry inside your
closed hand.
                    Shadowy thin, lovely,
your mother Meena grew even thinner.
Down to the slightest of her selves,
she fled the hospital room where
her father lay dying. She stepped off
the window's ledge and into her own
lonely death.
                    You and my son prepare
to nest in sleep, spoon to spoon.
But not before you bring me
an armful of plush animals
from your bed, tucking them
next to my pillow, nestling them
close. For me,
the mother who sleeps on her side
like a child, her body
curled into nothing
but itself.
                    Holy day, this day
now ending. From within the hollowed
mother-body, another body is born.
A mother's embrace breaks
and breaks open until
what's smallest lies—
like the speck of seed within
a fruit's stone—
                    whole and alone.

ON HEARING ABOUT
THE FEMALE EARWIG

Only now do I learn you could fly away—
with perfectly workable wings that lie hidden,
folded in tiny cases. But no matter.
You won't move from your eggs.
For weeks the thread of your tongue
licks each milky oval, keeping
the cluster of pale fruit
safe from infection.
                        A child, I'd heard—
from your very name—the threat.
While I slept in darkness, unaware,
you would seek out the moist canal of my ear,
your pincered body then hidden inside me,
gathering gleam from that passageway's
amber wax.
                I begged my parents to keep me
from ever falling asleep on the scatter
of fallen leaves where you lived. Turning back
a corner of sun-bleached percale on my bed,
they soothed, "Never mind, never mind.
You mustn't believe whatever
you hear."
                Hatched, your nymphs huddle
under the burnished chain
of your body. When they later stray
every which way into the leaf mold,
you bring them back to seek
the wet feast of decay, guarding them
until they've each cast two sets
of binding skin.
                        My own children grew up
alongside rows of sibilant sweet corn
rising an inch a day. The silk spurting

from each ear held one or two
of your kin in its tangle of threads.
"There" I said to my daughter, to my son,
"must be the reason for their name.
Those are the ears where they live"—
and yet, I knew my own Nana had seen
a kitchen that harbored your kind
as dirty, so pressed each earwig she saw
into a dark stain with a quick
plummet of thumb.

                After your labors
have seen the moon lose its husk of light
not once, but twice, you die,
exhausted. Your body then the bread
of your children's last meal
before they take their
separate ways.

              My parents and their parents
are decades dead. Each day my children
move farther beyond what I can give them.
I grow old knowing little. Never
could I have dreamed I'd find myself
being drawn to you—*your story*
having found,

           at last,

               its way to my ear.

IN THE CHURCH OF THE METAMORPHOSIS

—Ermoupolis, Greece

Old woman sitting beside me, you smell
of unwashed female. Even incense swung
from the priest's censor—that oily loft of musk—
masks none of your rankness as you rise
to kiss the glass that covers an icon's
gold-embellished face.
                                    Old one, you pull
the same coin out of your black pocketbook
ten times, then a key on its gray string ten more.
Mumbling, you cross back and forth
between your chair and the votive holder
to light one thin taper after another, to make
the sign of the cross onto your dark bodice,
returning to question me—in the Greek
I do not understand—about house keys
and offerings.
                        Who will ease from you
the frayed slip, the stained underpants,
and cast them away? Someone must steady you
as you step into a tub, must say to you, "Sit down,
Old Mother, into this warm water, rub soap
into your skin, into all the places," as I did
with my own addled mother, after
my father's death.
                            When he was dying,
she'd hugged me, saying, "Oh Honey,
isn't it strange, we've changed places, it's like
I'm the little girl now, you've become
the mommy," and—for the first time—
I had breathed in the sharp shock of her
unwashed body and clothing, the stink
of confusion and loss.

                    I could not help the vast
and hollow place that opened within my chest
the days after my father died. But I could
help my mother—the new widow,
raw and transformed—
to shower. "Try this soap, Mom.
Geranium, such a pretty color.
Lather, rub it everywhere, between
your legs, up into your crotch,
you mustn't forget
to wash there."
                    Old woman in this church
foreign to me—its cerulean domes
spangled with stars, haven
my mother would have gladly traveled
half the world to see—
someone must tend you.
One of us must hold you dear,
must bend to wash away
the unholy smell wafting
from your time-sullied self.
Some daughter must dare
                        to mother you.

AT THE FOSTER HOME

—for my mother

The food you just ate is a simple nothing,
its name and taste swallowed by a ravenous mouth
not your own. You say the meal was fine,
"just fine," then minutes later ask me
when you're going to finally get
something to eat.
                The easiest to remember,
I am the one you fear has forgotten you—
my daily visits gone minutes after
I kiss you goodbye. Each day you ask me
where I'm going. Every day you ask me to please
explain where you're staying. You tell me again
you're being "a good girl"—ashamed when you
can't remember where the bathroom is, stunned
then subdued to see your bedroom set, clothes,
and family portraits appear from behind
an unfamiliar door. You accept with only a wince
your belongings shrunk to what a single room
in a stranger's house can hold.
                              Yours isn't even
a casting away—no knitting needles, bridge decks,
or driver's license knowingly laid to one side,
then to be remembered and mourned. The victim
who wanders in shock through a ransacked life,
you stare at vacant spots, unable
to even guess
                what once was there.

PASSAGE

A favorite student brought snapshots
to show me. His trophies. There, he pointed,
it was him hunkered behind his first bobcat,
his fingers lifting its head by tufted ears
so the camera could get a good shot.
And there he was with a brace of mallards,
his hand circling their necks, their bodies
hanging from his grip like two
swollen sacks.
                And there. He was standing
in front of his family's small cinder-block house,
grinning. Before him, in a V, he'd arrayed
seven Canada geese, laying them breast down
on the pale thatch of November lawn.
He'd pried their wings open, into motionless flight.
Straightened each neck. Pointed each of their bills
in the camera's direction, toward
some spot just out of sight,
dead ahead.
                Long ago, when a boy first took
an animal's life, elders marked his forehead
with a smear of the slain creature's warm blood—
him not yet a man, a son whose mother
could only step back and watch his new life
begin to unfold.
                No daughter ever carried
such a mark. If only I could return
to a morning of my thirteenth year.
With my first menstrual blood I'd mark
my forehead not once, but twice.
First for the life I'd just lost.
Again for that life I would make
from loving such boys, such men—
my animal life
                just beginning.

ii. Outbound Messages

A BLUEPRINT OF THAT VASTER BLUE

Within this city built from patterns
intricate as the mapping of stars, I gaze
out my open window and see
two young women—unfamiliar to me—
holding hands as they walk along, leaning
into each other.
                    In a world where ancient cities
mirrored what little we knew of heaven's
own architecture, I hear the two women speak
to an old neighbor lady crossing the street.
They tell her enough of something
about the sweet wiles of false spring
to make the old woman laugh.
Her head held down
by the curve of her spine, she smiles
as she bumps a chrome walker
up and over the curb.
                        From inside this house
deep within a sidereal plan, I watch
the redheaded boys from across the way
chalk basketball plays on squares of sidewalk—
a white-lined map of drives and blocks
for the hoop set at regulation height
above the street outside their house.
Clustered, their X's and looping arrows
emerge like the roughed-in record
of a constellation caught
in motion, a world they people
with cartoon musclemen at war—
slam-dunking, bursting
through a rim.

                May those young women
be lovers, their mouths graced with the salt
of that joy. May they marry
and become a child's two mothers.
May their family of three choose
to live nearby—on the corner,
in that blue house now for sale,
their front garden blooming with starts
of snowdrop, poppy, purple iris
carried to them in welcome by us,
their neighbors.
                May the redheaded boys'
inevitable taunts and shoves give way
to an easy thonk thonk of a ball on asphalt.
May their chalk warriors melt
at next rain. The boys, may they play
far into summer evenings—their bodies
crossing through and beyond
the stark boundary of that painted key,
white on dark pavement.
For all comers,
                let them make room.

ON THIS SIDE OF THE RIVER

—for Kyoko Nakai

Heading away from your funeral,
in the car I hear the kind of talk you'd expect—
memories of you, the dead-end questions
begun with *There isn't really any answer,*
but why, why? and I'm quiet,
thinking of your face leaning
into that magnolia bloom I'd brought
to my classroom, your beauty
a match for the sharply perfumed
cream of its petals.
                Easy curves, and now
a straightaway where the little highway takes
its course a bit uphill of the river.
On the long stretch between bridges,
nothing crosses the river for miles
either way.
              I'm mostly silent, and more so
when I look out my window at a mown field
stretching up from the river's bank
to meet the shoulder of this busy road.
I quicken, staring. A lone heron
stands in the grass. Neck stretched and straight,
head exactly still, near enough to eye me—
if it cared to. Close enough it's a shock to me
who's never seen anything
in these shorn fields but smears
of blackbirds.
           Heron. This close
to streaming traffic, on this particular day.
The same Great Blue Heron who—
in oldest stories making their way,
through time, toward me—carries the dead

onto a farther shore, safely from this side
to the next. A *psychopomp*, a soul–guide
is here, beside this highway
I'll travel tomorrow, then time after
time after. Each day, I'll strain
for another glimpse, as I drive
the very route taking me away
from you now, speeding me
along
        to a place of another crossing.

ELEGY, 1980

—for Dane Young, 1949-1979

Pine-lengths I carry
from a lodgepole thicket
scrape bits of pitch into my skin.
The inside of my arms
will be red and swollen
long after this firewood is split
and stacked away.
                          You too were out
gathering wood that day last fall.
Coaxing your dog Razorback
out of the way, to safety, you were
crushed by a falling tree.
Where I sit resting against a pine,
wild strawberries grow
in profusion, staining the duff
with half-hidden fruit.
                          You taught
Paradise Lost to milltown children,
your classroom reeling when Lucifer
took flight. One boy still boasts
of reading Milton. He carries
his knowledge like an awkward badge,
recalling the gleam
of fallen angels.
                          You knew everything
driven to a forest floor
would find its way into air again.
Wood smoke pluming a winter sky.
Your voice held fast
in a millworker's thoughts
as he pulls his shift—sweet resin
thick in his breath—him guiding
lengths of pine
                          on their way.

ONE CHANCE

*—after filling out a Teacher Assessment of Suitability for Army
Special Schools for Tony Herrara and dropping it into the mail slot*

The form had asked me to please rate,
on a scale of 1 to 5, the applicant's
MENTAL STABILITY.
GENERAL HEALTH.
RESPECT FOR AUTHORITY.
                                    He called me
Sweetpea once, his words surprising himself
more than anyone else. Everybody in class
laughed, especially me. Tony was pleased,
smiling slowly, his tongue tasting
the sour metal of new braces.
HONESTY.
DEPENDABILITY.
ABILITY TO LIVE IN CLOSE
PROXIMITY TO OTHERS.
                            When I stepped
between Monte and James, Tony stepped too,
barely touching Monte's arm, talking fast
to Monte about suspension, getting grounded,
cooling off, while I was talking
James out the door.
DILIGENCE.
POTENTIAL FOR LEADERSHIP.
INITIATIVE.
                    A shepherd-mix wandered
into class during finals, one blue eye,
one brown. Tony borrowed my mug
for a water bowl, and although others
coaxed and whistled, it chose
to sleep by his desk. When the dog
grew restless, Tony lifted it in his arms,

carried it the length of the hall
before setting it down
on the grass outside.
                              Tony's Assessment Form
on its way to the Army, I suddenly recalled
another boy, Jeremy, back at school one day,
discharged early after a scrape with a sergeant,
his hunger for action as persistent
as the florid tattoo on his arm.
Hair shorn, fatigues blade-creased,
Jeremy had pulled a desk up to mine to talk,
believing I was—besides himself—
the only one in that classroom
who wasn't a child.
"Got trained to run a million dollar
laser weapon. For tanks. I can hit one
a mile away. Zap a hole in it
just an inch wide. Heats up
what's inside to 5,000 degrees.
Sucks everything through
the hole out the back. Boom.
It's done. But tanks cost
big bucks. They only let me try it
on one."
                    I wanted Tony's form back
from the Army, so I could tell
one other truth. Just one.
Yes, Antonio Herrara wants to be
among those few you'll choose,
wants the chance to wear
your special uniform. But what
you hope I'll praise in Tony
will make him
                              unfit to serve.

ADMISSION

We'd paid to see an elephant handler
shout "STEADY STEADY" to his charge
as he slipped a garbage can under
the stream of urine, another under falling dung
so deftly he didn't miss a word of his patter.
The oval path remained unspotted, we watchers
broke into applause, and the child who rode
the elephant's back—her sandals brushing its hide,
pale coral speckled with charcoal—was pleased
by the part she'd played.
                            We'd paid to watch
polar bears swing their blond heads from side to side,
casting for a fleck of scent—perfume, menses, sweat,
the meat on our breath—while two guys jostled
at the rail, one growling "Shit, Randy, that she-bear
wants your body. She's spotted your beard,
Dickface."
                 I watched a beautiful woman
in black and white polka-dot shorts
stare at the bat-eared fox who did nothing
but, with nose down, dig dig dig
trying to make an escape route
near the edge of its concrete moat—
a spot between its obsidian eyes rubbed raw
from the attempts to tunnel its way free.
The woman's skin, flawlessly pale, was marked
by a large mole on the back of one thigh—
darkest mole. Small black
                            animal burrowing out.

STORYTIME

An out-of-season perfume
chokes February's air. Hyacinth. Narcissus.
Fragrant flowers of ancient myth, they murmur
their stories of grief and regret.

                                Hyacinth sprang
from the blood of a friend heedlessly slain.
Narcissus was born from the blindness
of self-absorption. Both now bloom too early
for even the bees, whose better instincts
keep them at home—
in decimated numbers.

                            These normally sodden
late weeks of winter unfold their preternatural tale—
page after page of dry, warm days having finally
given us pause. This *once upon a time* is a strange one
filled with sinking water tables. A raw earth
lies exposed, chapters from a shoreline's past
that have never—in our memory—
seen light before.

                        Ours is the story
of the woodsman getting his wish, a magic axe
falling trees without pause—the hills in his wake
scabbed and bald. Ours is a tale of dragons—
sour beasts gone crazy to own what little gold
they don't already hoard. The fable
of Greed's Coronation, of Wisdom's Exile,
is our own—a plot whose ending
we know.

                Now we begin to listen,
each word settling in to unsettle us
as if we'd never heard it before.
Already we feel ourselves gone
speechless, our throats

                        tight with thirst.

BELATED

Janice Nakata, May Fete Queen,
Honor Roll girl, I'm glad I was once
your sister—if only in a high school club
playing 1950's grownup with our bids
and blackballs and pledge week,
our pale organza formals, our long
white gloves.
                    Janice with skin the color
spun from wild honey, did you wince
at me?—the tall thin one blotched by moles
and imperfection, admiring in silence
your sweet-spoken ways, your darkest eyes
that met our eyes with only
kindness.
                    I must have thought we'd all
grown up much like me, with a father
exempt from the army because he worked
in the shipyards, a father left at home
to weld, sealing those giant hulls
bound for Pacific seas—a daddy free
to build his daughter a wooden stepstool
that exact size so she could reach
the bathroom sink to brush her teeth, a dad
who could drive her to see grandparents
in their gabled house just across
our tree-shaded city.
                    Janice Nakata,
Beautiful Sister, I ask you now
what I did not know to ask you then.
Tell me.
                    Where—in which
makeshift barrack shadowed by
high barbed wire—did we imprison
your family
                    during the war?

WERE I TO PAINT YOUR BEAUTIFUL EYEBROWS

—for Tess Gallagher

> *We play wine games*
> *And recite each other's poems.*
> *Then you sing, "Remembering South of the River"*
> *With its heartbreaking verses. Then*
> *We paint each other's beautiful eyebrows...*
>
> —Wu Tsao

Because yours are startled birds caught
in flight above your eyes, high catches of sky,
rounded cornices shading the windows
of your open gaze, I'll first need to learn
how to hold a brush away from its supple bristles,
my arm at a right angle to the brush's shaft—
a soft-tipped staff for making those curves
that cross the Irish meadow
of your brow.
                    That lesson will surely take me
a month. Then the stroke itself. Temple arch.
Meander's bend. Half a cordate leaf's rising swell,
its dip, its skimming off at the end.
For two months more, using clear water,
I'll practice this shape—no need to rush
my urge to see the results.
                    Another three to learn
the grinding of ink. Sienna, I'm thinking.
Or perhaps a dark brown flecked
with cinnabar's gleam, something to match
the long hair I remember pell-melling
down your back, Ray sitting beside
your empty chair, him holding

your gussy hat in his lap while you
read us your poems.
                         Another five to try ink
first on paper, then on my kitchen counter,
on the slats of each window's Venetian blind.
Thousands of red-glinted practice eyebrows
will fill my house. As many up-flung songbirds
as the pairs of wings veering into and out
of your poems. Across the lintel
of my front door. Above what will open
to welcome you, on that day
of your return. Slicing the air
with their high and lambent cries,
a whole covey
will wait—
                   caught in painted flight.

BLOOD TIE

—for Linda

Each grain of marrow's been scoured
out of your bones. Your core's been harrowed
with enough poison to leave you to teeter
on death's threshold—all this, so you can be given
a pint of your sister's stem-cells, the sister who shied
from giving them up to you.
                                        This gleaning
from a reluctant blood begins to graft.
Your gut says no with a scorn worlds beyond
any sister's disdain. In flat-out refusal, your body
rebels, rejecting her cells. Food in,
and within minutes, shit out. Your system
empties itself, then—without pause—
begins to empty again.
                                        To calm your body's alarm,
you're given a recipe of drugs, then another
of liquid sustenance—both into a vein, drop by drop.
Nothing but this for weeks and days. Overseen
by machines counting on tallies precise and minute,
you say, "I must teach my body how to be
mine, teach it how to eat again"—
your body that's being slowly remade
by the seeds a sister begrudged
giving to you.
                        To help yourself learn
to eat, you try a bit of a staple food
that sustains blood-siblings the world around—
sisters who get along, those who don't.
You and this sister alive in your body
start over. Today, you two share
a first, a single
                        scant teaspoon of rice.

SPECIAL NEEDS

Special. Because she needn't
sing a note. Her specialty being
unneeded antic gesture—the at times
right-in-rhythm wave and flap of her hands,
the at other times out-of-sync swoop and pump
of her arms, those tilts, those bobs of her head.
Pulses of joy. Her constant ecstatic motion.
A sung note from her, now and again?
Perhaps. No one can tell.
                              One wild
smile after another, she holds her place
on the riser's third tier. In the all-girl
Fernwood Middle School Choir
she's a member
in good standing.
                    Who would say
she doesn't belong? Not the twenty-two
other girls who specialize in keeping
their eyes straight ahead on their director,
on her gesturing arms. They lip-read
their leader's mouth as she swiftly forms
a lyric's words. She models the script
her girls strictly follow. Their part
is to stay aligned with the song, regardless
of outbursts from the girl who attends
no regular classes, the one
needful of special care.
                          Between two numbers,
the girl shouts out a bit of needling impatience,
anxious to get to the next number.
The director laughs, quips aloud,
"She's said what's on all our minds!"
Stretching her arms toward her group,
she coaxes them into the first notes

of "I See the Light," while that girl's
upper body jolts into charades
of the lyric.
                    On cue from their leader,
the twenty-two have given the twenty-third
their gift. They make room for the odd one
by not giving way to her distractions—
the only possible way this
Special Needs girl could,
with their choir,
                    stand and sing.

A PROOF

—for Adrienne Rich, Stanford, 1987

Poli-Sci 161. In this borrowed hall,
from its lectern, you offer us
your proof. Headed home
on Route 13, you'd been caught
in the past week's front-page storm,
fists of wind pounding and slamming,
the asphalt slash
fast becoming a river,
your car a bubble of steel
ready to float.
                You'd been desperate
for something to keep it steady.
Something more than smart driving.
"Poems," you tell us, "I recited
as many as I could remember.
Coleridge, Wordsworth, Elizabeth Bishop,
loud against that rain, that wind.
Line after line, mile upon mile.
Into that din. And—see—
it worked. Truly, it did.
I'm here!"
            Behind and above you,
chalkboards rise to the ceiling, looming
with words left from a lesson
on the science
of current affairs—
   DETERRENCE
    SURVIVABLE LAUNCH
DEFENSIVE INTENT
               —words not meant
to get *anyone* home.

But you did,
you're smiling, and we smile back,
despite what hangs over us all.
You bring us that news
found only in poems.
You call on us to know
right words, in a right order.
To speak aloud
          what we know by heart.

YOUR GLASS FACE IN THE RAIN

*—at the Los Prietos Forest Service outdoor display
honoring William Stafford, 2013*

My fingertips wipe fine rain
from your 1940's snapshot face, off your T shirt,
stark white in that day's sun. I wipe mist
from your chino pants—their rolled-up cuffs,
the telltale rip exposing one knee. I take soft downfall
away from your half-laced canvas shoes
and note how they're set steadfast
on grassy ground.
                              Here, oaks live and have thrived
for a long into longer time. Inside the Ranger Station
close by, a botanical poster claims
among California's nineteen oaks,
the Oracle Oak is a wide-spread hybrid.
But the Ranger tells me, "Not so. Oracles
are rare." I agree.
                              Today's rain collects
on this plaque recounting your service
as a C.O., holding your young image and a single
early daybreak poem, one of the hundreds
you wrote in the time you were here,
exiled from the world at its war. I watch
this moment's rain sag over the weathered barrack
behind you—long-gone building where you
would sleep for most of this
photograph's night.
                              Some forty years later—
writing a morning's poem—you would follow
a thread and foretell what today I see come true:
to the place where you once lived, *for those
who remember well, there will come
a glass face, invisible but still and real,
all night outside in the rain.*

From this monument's
clear surface, again I wipe away newly fallen drops.
The trunks of nearby oaks gleam darkly. Their leaves
shoulder the sky's weight with barely a sigh.
I look once more at your eyes, your face.
Today's rain gathers to streak
over this photo's grass growing thick
from Prietos earth—the ground
where I now see you
                    taking your stand.

HOME ADDRESS

—for William Stafford

Locals say you seemed unlikely
for a famous guy. They'd see you at Wizer's,
at Safeway buying milk, and long ago,
in the old library—that cubbyhole of shelves
in the police station's back room.
That was before the new library opened
on 4th, the one you dedicated
with a poem.
                    You'd be walking along
or pedaling your bike, a rucksack on your back,
your gaze ready to meet each person
as a "separate, luminous being."
Making a point to talk with strangers,
you turned newcomers into new friends.
Then, "So long"…and you were
on your way.
                    Neighbors watched their kids
cartwheel across the grass with yours,
while you and Dorothy planted the cedars
that would one day shelter your house
with forest-shade. *All* the nearby kids
grew up as your next-door neighbors.
From September to June, they whooped and ran
not far from your backdoor—
on the playground of the grade school
where Dorothy taught.
                    At the post office,
folks bumped into you sending off
your batches of poems, or replies to the mail
that had reached you just hours before.
Across each envelope's upper left,
in your bold upright hand, you wrote

Sunningdale Road, Lake Oswego.
On every outbound message,
your signal was clear:
                    this is home.

A HEART'S ECHO

—*for Dorothy Stafford, my pacifist friend*
  whose middle name was Hope

In black and white your heart's image
swelled and fell, its valve a flap
again then again flung open.
The technician shifted his machine's view
to record and gauge. After twenty years
away in the Navy, he was home. For good.
You asked him when the wars would end.
He answered, "In Iraq, soon. Afghanistan,
who could know."
                        I'd known your heart's work
for years, how its wisdom schooled
anyone who'd listen. Watching
a bright line scrawl its beat
across a screen, I asked the technician
how much of what he was able to measure
a doctor could detect with a mere stethoscope.
More than I might imagine. "Some ears,"
he said, "learn to hear better than
any machine."
                        I imagined an ear laid
against your chest, learning. I thought
of the four babies who grew for months
in your womb, listening, fed by
your heart's pulse. Moment to moment
they each, in turn, learned nothing less
than goodness—how to echo
the steady sound of
                        peaceful striving.

THE ONE AROUND WHOM STRANGERS WEAVE AND CLING

—for Ken

I wait. A long time I spend waiting.
Old and just older men walk by
the Paris park bench where I sit.
One by one. None are you. No you
to tell me why you've been gone
this long.
        I can guess. You've been waylaid
by the Roma. You're learning—quick—
to speak their tongue. The women
keep paper money tucked in lace bras.
Coins loose in deep skirt pockets.
The better to jangle. Gold and silver bangles
shinny up their dark forearms. Their men
pour whisky onto graves. At least onto graves
of Papas and Gypsy Kings.
        A wind blows dust
across this park's ground. While a few dead leaves
fly, trees shudder into late June greenery.
Chestnuts that bloomed long before I was here
bear pale burrs. No you.
        OK. I can see
how many young women are pushing babies
in strollers across every acre of the park.
They all must pay you their respects—many,
too many, beautiful enough to make
tears crowd your eyes. One smells of lemon.
Another, musk. Magnolias have opened
their white globes on branches close enough
to touch. Turns out, I bet, a brunette
who could easily be Turkish
has named her baby your name.

How could you not stop to talk with her?
This beauty's own name sort of somewhat
rhymes with mine. But explaining that to her
would surely take even more time
than you've already taken. You make
the two-second decision to leave me
out of the conversation.
                              Could be, you've
encountered a man alone at a chess board.
He has Bobby Fischer's book
My Sixty Memorable Games open to page 52.
He's enough at loose ends to agree to a game.
He scorns speed-chess. Disdains
wearing a watch. You've met
the perfect partner.
                              I wait into the next plane
of long belief, noting the movement
of leaf-shade across mown grass.
My own sundial. Parisian sunlight leaps off
thick gray hair of a man headed this way.
Not you.
                              Most likely, an Algerian roustabout—
another of your newly minted friends—
catches up with you as you walk. You've decided
it's past time to return to me. You ask him
for directions. He nods in reply. With a pencil stub
he slides out of his shirt pocket, he draws
a map on a scrap of paper. Excitement rises
from his runes into your eyes. He licks the lead.
You peer and accept his route as your fate. You know
that X marking your destination lies at least
one more stranger
                              shy of where I wait.

DIVINE INTERVENTION

—for Ken

i.

Nearly 55. Headlong in love. With you.
In hunger to learn your every way and by-the-way,
I rushed to read the Victorian novel you touted,
you cherished—and came to its end that drops
out of a sky blue enough to be
transparent. At the last possible heartbeat,
love arrives to save the novel's hero.
The one mistreated, maligned.
Deus ex machina, and I knew you'd swallowed—
without a catch of doubt—nothing less
than a miracle to right the story's wrongs.
I turned its last page, queasy with misgiving,
afraid you believed a happy ending
not humanly possible, fearing
you might distrust
                    any good end.

ii.

A cruel mother begins the story you call
your own. In her reign over your young life,
she exacts—with each scalding screech,
every fisted blow—her toll. She one day
locks you, ten years old and naked,
outside the house. Leaves you to quake in cold,
in shame. A year or so later, inches from your eyes,
she tears into shreds what you've propped on the altar
of your bedroom windowsill, the baseball cards
you've sorted and savored so often
you can recite their litanies of stats and dates.

Each havoc at her hands becomes
a small indelible death. No rescue appears—
divine or not—to save your childhood
from this darkest of queens.
                        To her, by the time
we met, you no longer even spoke. You dismissed
her wheedling letters with an off-hand scoff.
From one of those missives, you lifted
what she'd enclosed, a photo
of herself, smiling. Before my eyes,
you ripped the image apart. She's been
dead now a good many years.
Best riddance, you say.
Yet she is the one
                        I fear the most.

           iii.

She and only she begins
The Story of You and Women,
that crowded, brambled tale wherein
I make my late entrance,
able to speak
only in present tense.
I can never love you enough
to undo—with any number of kisses—
a Fell Mother's work. My kiss
holds no magic, I know.
And to yearn for such rescue
asks too little. I want
much more.
                        I believe in
the all too improbable
miracle of kindness. Nothing else
will do. A lesser god than that?
I refuse. This is—after all—
                        my story, too.

iii. Small Suns

GRACE

—remembering Katrina

A continent away from my ocean-cooled
Northwest home, a hurricane's flood made refugees
of thousands, homes and buildings shattered
then ground into a slurry of slash
dotted with corpses.
                        Bodies floated in turgid rivers.
Iridescence swirled across the water's heat-gleamed surface.
Thousands of miles from that flood, different thousands
starved in drought-scoured lands, each face
seething with flies.
                        Does dew still fall in places
crazed by drought? Does it, at first light, wet
a single tongue? Is *any* drop of flood-water safe to drink?
I sip a cup of sweetened tea. Not even the smallest mishap
here, where for two days in a row, a hummingbird
comes to the nearby dahlias—their red
a match in all but iridescence
for its throat.
                For a second day, a hummer,
Little Holy One, comes close enough to set up
a tremor behind and below my ears, in those skull-bones
created to catch, to thrum with sound.
                                        A hum sets in
under my brain that's filling again
with footage of bleary people walking in lines
on broken roads, what they can save slung
on their backs in plastic garbage sacks. Today
and the day before, a ruby-throated
spirit visits here. In my favor,
for no particular reason,
                        a small god intervenes.

WITH CHRISTMAS SEASON
HARD UPON US

—on Ari Folman's film Waltz with Bashir

In the restaurant window, a sign.
LEBANESE COOKING. Inside,
a glitzy fir tree my husband wants near him.
For the evergreen scent. The tree turns out to be
a fake. We sit by it anyway,
inches from its glittering cheer.
"A typical Middle Eastern decoration," he quips.
Our waitress replies, "We're Christians,"
then names her Lebanese Catholic Church
a few blocks away.

                      The moussaka, baba ganooj,
and falafel please us. Learning a Middle Eastern Church
is nearby—the chance for Holy Land borders
to be blurred and erased—
gladdens me.   .
              Home early enough for a movie,
we watch a former soldier unravel amnesia,
his chronic nightmare stalling my breath as he floats
face up in a coppery sea. Israeli, he knows
he was at Sabra and Shatila. There in Beirut.
For the massacres. Knows, yet remembers
nothing. Then finally recalls himself
feeding flares into a launcher's maw.

                          Red suns ooze
through a black sky. The Israeli soldiers light the way
for Lebanese Christians to push refugee children, women,
old men—like chains of paper dolls—up against walls.
Palestinians with their arms splayed, with palms and faces
flattened into stucco.

More than a quarter century later,
safe at home, I watch on a screen, seeing those Christians
fire the rifles. As many rounds as it takes.
An extra to be certain.
                              This Christmas I want
a real tree. I too like evergreen. Nothing less
than the haunted sting of resin in my breath
will suffice for such a holy time.
Balsam was the balm daubed onto wounds
in our own Civil War. *Christian soldiers.*
At Sunday School I sang *Onward!* to them,
just as I'd been taught.
                              Baby Jesus, Prince of Peace,
your birthday tree is a pagan relic. For this sacred season,
only its dark
                    underworld scent will do.

OFFERINGS

For morning prayer this December day,
I stare at an image of Lord Ganesh,
the elephant-headed god, lover of sweets.
Even his pet rat nibbles on a golden candy
clawed from a mounded bowl.
A flower garland sheds petals
onto his knotted rug.
A five-flamed lamp sets off
its tiara glow.
                    I'm too fat already for even
the smallest mountain of sugar.
My North American winter garden scoffs
at swelling buds. The tiara I own
is a joke-gift, cheap sparkler
bought for me from a mall's kiosk
that caters to each princess
of a prom.
                    Nowhere in my Episcopal
Book of Common Prayer did a god crave
sweets. On not a single page did a deity
possess more than two arms.
The Virgin Mary was not a goddess.
Our Deacon warned against believing that.
In no prayer did Mary do
what Lakshmi does—one pair
of her goddess hands raised to hold
two blown blooms of lotus.
No words writ Episcopalian
allowed third and fourth arms
to drop along her sides, those palms
open, gold coins flowing
from each.
                    That's abundance, not money,
streaming from Lakshmi's fingertips.

The lotus is her many-wicked
flower, sprouting its rosy anther-flames.
Her sari is pure silk, her bangles
precious.
                    My *Book of the All Too Common*
was small, bound in black pebbled paper.
Meant to resemble leather, that cover
crumbled under years of my touch.
Little enough, it fit into the slightest of my
childhood hands.
                        Are those coins cold
when they emerge on Lakshmi's palms?
Do they cool her fingers as they fall?
At her temple, hands of Lakshmi's devotees
offer—to her jeweled and gilded idol—
folded pieces of tacky spangled cloth
meant to look like priceless saris she might
someday wear.
                    The quarter I clutched
for the church offering dish grew warmer
each minute within my left hand's
lesser grip. Even then, my childhood's
two-bit coin was never
purely silver.
                    At any Temple of Ganesh,
worshippers offer trays mounded
with cheap confections, the priest
sliding them toward Ganesh's huge statue,
so close their rims touch
his plump pink toes.
                        I once stared and stared
at the staked and bleeding feet of Jesus
as he hung on the cross above the altar—
so tendoned, so narrow, so thin.
In another world, I might have offered him
something to ease his anguish.
A *sweetmeat*.

       The body of Christ lay
dry and wan on my tongue,
his blood an acrid echo
in my breath.
           I said my prayers.
My *Most Common Book* sprouted
a thin, black—and surely not silk—
ribbon to make certain
             I kept my place.

LUNAR NEW YEAR

—Portland, in a time of war

Last night, at a friend's house, the feasting.
Local pinots. Long string beans dry sautéed,
garlic-rich. Small balls of chewy dough
that hid tart plum hearts. A coconut pudding
stiff enough to slice into translucent
moon-slivers. But before the food,
some poems.
              The first, read by a woman
who announced she'd earlier searched
the Internet, hoping to find a Chinese poem
mentioning wine. She did. Others recited
Liu K'un and Tu Fu. Then Li Po, poet of exile,
who—in the company of mountains—
found his peace. And last, I read
the poem I'd chosen, Lao-tzu's verse
on war.
          On my front porch, this day's paper
arrives with no room for Lao-tzu to tell us
"Weapons are the tools of violence;
all decent men detest them." No feature
quotes the ones who might "…enter a battle
gravely, with sorrow and with great compassion,
as if attending a funeral."
                            The street is lit
with the broken shine of rain. Obscured
by our city's house-clad hills, Mt. Hood
rises nearby. I know that even unseen,
its white slopes gleam
like that wisdom found
in an ancient poet's verse.
                            Inside, I set the paper
beside the party favors I left scattered

on the table last night. The Red Envelope
rests alongside its contents: a meal ticket
to offer the next someone who begs on the street,
a few foil-covered chocolate coins.
And in their midst, that most auspicious
of New Year gifts.
                        I pick it up, a bit
of good fortune I hold in my upturned palm.
A single Mandarin orange—
bright as
            a longed-for sun.

ARRANGEMENTS HAVING
BEEN MADE

—"Not to worry. A driver will meet you at the Mumbai airport."

Eager Indian men in a line. Each held—
collarbone-high—a piece of paper bearing
a hand-scripted, computer-printed,
consonant-ridden Indian name
into whose pronunciation
I knew whole syllables
would disappear.
                        In a row of strange faces,
each one chinning itself on an even
stranger name, every pair of eyes
met my own with the strangest
of unspoken queries,
Are you mine?
                        The one who held up
a piece of paper bearing the apparition
of my spelled-close-enough name,
he was the one I followed
as he pushed my baggage trolley
into that cool season's
hot night.
                        Some man appeared
from within the swarm of too similar,
all too unfamiliar men to offer me
my name. I went with him into
an unknown city, into silence
of unshared language, for the long ride
by palaces, skyscrapers, paan huts,
chawls, him driving me off
in a direction as easily
dead wrong as not.

                    And I barely
teetered toward terror. All because
he held up to my eyes a sign calling out
one given name, mine entirely.
Followed by a marriage name,
in any entirety, not.
Simply because his sign
bespoke a pair of words—
only those two—
I concede as being
                    who I am.

HAND INTO HAND

—Hyderabad, India

Through the pale powder of excrement
emptied from pigeons teeming on each perch
this shrine offers, I come walking
barefoot to the tomb
at Mecca Masjid.
                          Bare-headed, but because
I come from a world far away, the keeper
allows me to enter. Without a scarf.
In need of the fine-hemmed cloth
that would cover
my swirls of curling hair.
                          Empty-handed too,
so from a shallow bowl atop
the Mehboob Ali Khan's tomb,
he takes a bit of marigold-bloom
and places it into my
wanting hands.
                          Having come here lacking
a bouquet to place on the Beloved One's tomb,
I am given a piece torn from an auspicious
flower's body. I then offer the Mehboob Ali Khan
its scent, its silk, this world's yellow dust.
The tomb-keeper—gray bearded, turbaned,
his eyeglass lenses the only part of him
not specter thin—blesses me with a touch
to my uncovered head from the long bouquet
of peacock feathers held
in his other hand.
                          His work—to fill
what arrived here empty so it could empty itself
again—is done. His Beloved, now honored.
Now satisfied.

                    Pigeon lime gathers
onto my soles in gray-white grit. Its acrid dust
crowds my breath. My bare feet move glyphs
of pigeon feather aside. Down eddies
ahead as I walk.
                    The flocks of Mecca Masjid
have shed what floats away before my every step.
This far world empties itself just long enough
to make room for my exact work,
the entering of each such
opened place.
                    Back at the marble stairs
where I came in, a shoe wallah watches
my gaping sandals for a price—
the 5-rupee coin that will fill hers,
make empty again
                    my hands.

FED

—in Safranbolu, Turkey

A bird, I would have to be the only
one-footed Turkish sparrow
among these I feed with bread saved
from the hotel's breakfast table.
Plain, hopping, atilt. I wouldn't be
the bird a bit smaller than the rest.
Not that petit dark-headed stranger
whose name, in even my own tongue,
I don't know. Not the one
who flies to this garden's edge
and stays for a minute or two—
scarved in sleek black,
tail in a constant
flit and shimmy.
                    More of a wren,
though not that small, it shifts this way,
then that, not even trying to reach
the crumbs scattered on stone paving,
keeping an eye on the lesser types who,
if they can—and the hobbled can't—
grab too many pieces at once.
Then, out of puddles left from someone
hosing the terrace early this morning,
they scoop water
into their throats.
                    I'd be a female sparrow,
of course, so even plainer—lacking
the sooty eye-swatch and ascot
of my brothers.
                    My swollen ankle will heal.
I'll forget this one-footed, clumsy hopping.
Walking again with even steps, I'll eat—
from the hands of strangers—
the dark
          bread of what I can reach.

THE TURNOVER

—*In the game Pictionary, one player of each pair is given the same
word. That one then draws a picture to prompt his or her partner
to utter the word first—rebuses, stick figures, diagrams, anything,
everything short of spelling it out.*

In that game a husband and wife were not
necessarily a team. That time, my husband and I
and my dearest friend each had *other* partners.
There, we three would compete.
                                    Our teams began
on even ground, but before I'd even touched
my pencil to paper, my best friend drew
a few sure lines, then turned what she'd drawn
upside down. Her partner looked and said,
"Capsize!" It was done.
                              In mere seconds
my friend had sketched the cup of a boat,
its mast and sail, the waving line of water.
Then, with a simple reversal,
she'd won.
                From my husband's voice came
the cry of my best friend's name,
its three syllables singing a whole refrain
of *How could anyone be so/ clever doesn't
begin to describe/ you really are/ my god
you are/ wonderful*—a sound that rushed
in less than a heartbeat from him to her
to him, then into the high color
flooding my friend's
delighted face.
                    Dazed, I applauded—
wondering why I didn't think of it first.
How could I have missed a thing so obvious,
been so easily outdone? Yet I had to give

my wonderful friend her due: it was
a perfect clue.
                    Most any fool but me
could see by then it was *m'aidez, m'aidez*—
the boat had tipped over and everyone headed
into the water.
                    Arms churned, legs pumped.
I choked and flailed, went under
and under, rising to glimpse my husband taking
steady determined strokes. Right beside him,
my dear best friend—even as she swam—
was still smiling, her face slick and shining,
knowing herself to be more than game.
She and my husband were
a team.
            They'd right themselves.
                            In no time.

HIS PLACE

From the next room I could hear
water running, a toothbrush working
against his fine, perfect teeth. A drawer
he opened, then closed, a pillow he plumped
and slid into a case. Where I sat, scattered
across a table belonging to this man I had
come to know, yet barely knew—
how could someone I'd known so briefly
have delved into my body that deeply?—
was spread the stuff of mystery,
his life.
                    To my right was a pile
of clippings from the *New York Times*,
wherein most of a long-lost universe
had been found, and a race horse
named Cigar was two victories short
of Citation's record.
                              A photocopied article
with a post-it note from one of his
would-be lovers put a reader "inside
the sexual crucible where
the thrill of connection
opens us to the terror
of loss and pain." She'd jotted to him
"pls read (if you're int'd)." The front door
opened, closed, he was out, he was in.
I noted a book about healing hearts.
And an article on the gender back-talk
in E. B. Browning's poetry
by a woman most likely
another former lover.
                              Away to my left
at the table's edge, sat
the two books of my poems

I'd given him.
Mine.
                Even in their cloth-rich covers,
they were suddenly pale, thin.
They lay on top of the love poem
I'd written to him when I'd known him
even less, the poem on a single
creamy sheet, opened,
spread flat, a few lines
showing.
                I could see my own words
sleep, breath, skin, but then my eyes
failed me, and he walked back into the room,
setting the healing hearts
onto the table again, repositioning
gender's back-talk.
                He was going
to bed, had turned out his light.
Waiting for me, or not waiting for me,
I could not tell. The blood red sheet
of Chinese paper I'd folded around
my poem for him
before I'd put it in the mail—
gift sent to him in the sweet
derangement of newest love—
that I could touch.
Did touch. That one
heart's pulse
                lay within my reach.

HALF THE TELLING

"Come here," he said, after I'd stared
for minutes at the leaf he'd taken me to see.
Just one on a night of a thousand thousand
still on branches or muddled against
the ground or suddenly into the brief
spiral of falling.
                But this leaf held itself
mid-air between the tree and ground,
just below our eyes' level. It hung
from an unseen spider-strand,
held aloft by what connected it
to another—suspended in this middle
of night's openly cold air,
but not in the least
held still.
             "Stand here," he said and then,
open armed, moved opposite me, taking
my hands in his, making of us a circle
surrounding the drifting,
flickerish leaf.
               Back and forth,
in languid loops, it pointed first to him,
then me with its pale stem. "Heart-high,"
I said as it found my chest with a touch
too light to feel, then it was back
to touch his chest as he said, "It's weaving
our hearts together, weaving your heart
into mine."
               It moved within the in-between
as a story will—weightless
between teller and listener. Joining.
Coming to stand behind me,
he pressed into my back and watched
as the leaf paused to skitter

against my lifted hand.
                              "What will we do…"
he began to ask, though he already knew
how I'd answer. This was, after all,
a telling of love—*our* love,
a tale veering back and forth
between episodes sweet and bitter.
And one telling is never
the whole story. "…Shall we leave it
alone or take it?" was his question.
I had to decide.
                              Out of thin air, I pulled
its levitation. That heart-weaver,
that artful pretender, this one
page of our story,
                              then in my hand.

SEMBLANCE

—two postmortem photographs, circa 1890

A newborn lying on a settee
covered with a darkly patterned
fringed scarf. This child in a white dress
twice the length of its body. Deep lace on the hem,
smocking at the yoke.
                              A christening gown.
The baby on its side, one arm under its head,
arm and head tipped up by a white pillow
embroidered in pale floss. The child's hand, tiny,
curving toward its temple—like a fluted,
half translucent shell.
                              Fine nose, fine mouth,
the eyes closed. Lids so thin they darken
into a soft smudge. Guise of sleep arranged
in a fashion an infant's body, alive,
would never choose.
                              I study two photos of this baby
hanging side by side in exhibit, one taken from perhaps
eight feet away, the other from much closer.
And then, I step toward
a closer look.
                              In one photo the pillow is plump,
barely dented by the weight of the newborn's head.
In the other, the pillow creases to cradle that elbow,
curving hand, that head. After arranging this baby
and taking a picture, someone had second thoughts,
rearranged it, and took the photo again. And yet—
its hair.
                              In the longer shot the newborn's hair—
what would have covered the pulse
at the soft-spot in its crown—is a dark,
distinct tuft. In the closer shot only an even fuzz
shadows its skull.

Two. Different babies,
their features almost identical, both dressed
in that long gown, laid out in that same strangely
adult way. Twins—dead within days, hours
of each other.
                    Or sister and brother born
a year or two apart and made to look the same by
what finery could be gathered for the sake
of memento, two made equal
by a photographer's art.
                              Someone prepares
the body for such an occasion. But no. Not
the mother. *Not her.* She waits with her family
in a nearby room.
                    The photographer takes—
from a fine blanket—that small body,
its skin smooth and cool as the skin of a rose.
He slides the dress over its head, threads
those tiny arms through the not much larger sleeves,
slumps the baby's head as he fastens the collar
at its back.
                    The sofa, the scarf, the pillow all ready,
he eases this slight weight down, arranges
the length of white fabric—the baby on its side,
one arm crooked under its head to soften
the neck's jarring angle, lace at the hem
pulled smooth, eyelids pressed down tight.
Impeccable repose.
                    He steps backward.
A last check. Mantling his head and shoulders
in black, he leans to the lens, studies the old,
odd jolt of a world suddenly lurched
upside down. Then waits for the blinding flash
to burn such thin
                    semblance of sleep away.

THE INDIGENOUS

Gone dreaming last night, I lost
my way. Again. Forgot it the second
I awoke with an old pop song
merry-go-rounding my mind. Hopeless.
But then I remembered it could be
I'm on a *trek* when I'm
dead to the world.
              In bygone times,
when Native people fell asleep, they left
their sprawling weight behind them
so they could take long journeys.
They said *dream* and meant
destiny too. They knew things.
                    They realized
a dry bone could hold a soul—a bird's bone,
or a mammal's emptied of marrow.
Drilled with holes, that bone could
make a flute. Air fooling around.
Some throat-wind caught
and set free to make a melody
that carried a soul.
              People who lived
long before me knew they needed to learn
one of the bone-flute songs. By heart.
Then journeying at night, they could purse
their lips and whistle that tune
each time they entered a ghost's
inverted world. They knew better
than to speak.
              Whistling warned the ghosts
that someone from the right-side-up
daytime world was near, one
who fretted about getting old, dying.
Whistling that song gave those people

a little edge, ghosts being deaf to shouts,
ghosts being given to sleeping all day,
then feeding on compost
all night.
                    Could *I* ever know enough
to tootle the right song
in my dreams?
                    The ghosts tolerated
those whistling, fretful folks.
Even pitied them a bit. Aging and death
didn't exist in the ghosts' topsy-turvy world—
they'd had quite enough of that already.
People who lived ages ago, they knew
how to call on a tune when it counted.
They'd learned how to sleep
their way into darkness
and back again.
                    Tomorrow I'll likely
awaken having forgotten to dream at all,
that brain-worm tune—the one I insisted playing
over and over when I was thirteen—
still tattooing its lyrics into my head.
Whatever I do—me being
whole generations past any soul-wind song—
won't be enough to help me.
Not even close.
Just me.
            Now.
                    Whistling in my dark.

OWL

—*Klamath Falls, 1982*

Pale and ghostly, one kind lives
in the long-abandoned barn
near the old farmhouse I call home.
These small specters raise their young
a few hundred feet from where
I try to rear mine. I am not
feathered in cream and tawn.
My face does not take the shape
of a heart. But I too fret
the tightness of my nest
and guard against my fledglings
leaving it too early. I see these birds
only when they—white phantoms—
glide from the barn at dusk.

By day

some great-horned ones
often roost on the poplar branches
hanging above our back yard.
Dark bronze giants,
they while away the late afternoon
watching me trim the grass, pull weeds,
scour the barbeque grill on the deck.
They keep track of our kitten as it plays
on the lawn, knowing if such
a ball of fur-covered fat were to scurry
at night, it could be had
in one swift swoop and strike.

Owl.

That name carried by both kinds
is a moan, a one-syllable
koan, a dominion of sound.
Its roundness rolls itself

only so far, then ends with my tongue
pressed tight against my mouth's roof.
As if enough has already
been said.
              Often I am alone
out back. When I raise my head, I see
the amber eyes of a raptor
staring at me. I know to remember—
from these days onward, into all my days—
I have been watched intently
by a wide-winged god. Grace
could hardly
              be more.

VOCATION

A purveyor of charms, I write
spells on pieces of paper, then give them
away. A spell to make honeybees not dwindle
in numbers. A spell to bless the red of dahlias that bring
bees flurrying to a garden. One to bless the wedding of two
women friends, each at the other's nectar-mouth. Another
to toast two men cloven together for twenty-five years.
A chant for seeds waiting to be buried so they can rise
again in leafy flourish. Songs for yeast bread.
For the bit of borrowed sun in an oven's heat.
Plain charms. Not so plain. Charms that require
the wind for translation.
                              Some people inform me
that no one will value what's given away. To them,
I'll present my bill. A dime per charm—enough to buy
pretty paper for more. Then I'll fashion the spell
that makes a dime payment enough to make
scoffers into believers.
                              I'll conjure a niggling charm—
one to keep those ants who yearn to live in my house
outdoors. Then a ring of words biting its own tail,
making the circle that keeps all crawling creatures
a-crawl. White magic spelled out
in black ink on a pale page.
                              On my list of spells-to-do,
I'll put a rabbit foot's worth of words to keep
loved-ones whole. Another for the balm called *healing*,
if my first attempt should fail. A charm to make the number
of sunlit hours and the time tomatoes need to ripen
come out even. An abracadabra so my husband avoids
the blind alleys of Wall Street. A sleight of hand to keep
my right hand writing. A wishbone inviting me
to make the tug from my side
so even, so steady,
                         the wish never needs to stop.

PERIODICAL

—a magazine also being, in fact, a storehouse for goods

The *Shambhala Sun* arrives
with today's mail to tell me I'm perfect
as I am, but I could still use a little work.
Early morning, and here I am again,
at work in these Buddhist fields of wisdom.
In newly arrived light, reading this *Sun*,
I find I can *be* a sun, not the clouds
that obscure it. Perfect.
                                    Inside the *Sun*
I've pulled up close to my nearsighted eyes,
sunlight seeps across polished wood floors
in the room where the Dalai Lama walks
on his treadmill—distant cousin
to the treadmill in my basement,
exercise machine I use pretty much
every day, but disdain. And I see
my disdain for what it is.
A cloud.
                        The Dalai Lama treads
the wide dark belt barefoot. One foot
a blur of motion. In the photo,
that forward-stepping foot is caught
as it comes down hard on its shadow—
the sun having come through vines
hanging from eaves to find its way through
the window into his exercise room.
A creature who knows her spiritual dawnings
to be both fitful and little, I realize I'm lucky
to be fit enough to use my dim-lit
basement device.
                        "Our Original Goodness"
is given a page of its own. I read it to see

if original goodness and I could ever be found
on the same page. I find that my foibles
are merely temporary, like the shadow
a cloud might cast. Good lord.
I'm already seventy-two. That's the long view
of impermanence. But I too am temporary.
My faults must be, ergo, ephemeral.
I guess I can call that
good news.
               I do, yes, I do want to be
that better person, me minus the clouds
called praise and blame. In my last dream
this earliest morning, mishearing what
a friend said, or not hearing it at all, I let
that missed hearing slide by. I pretended
to understand. A big mistake. My friend
got heat-flushed angry at me.
                        The *Sun* tells me
to stop making things worse. To simply
become the however-better-me
I long to be. It says to look for something
small, find something large.
                        OK. In my dream,
I cry. My friend cries. Yet she lets me circle her
in my arms. She doesn't shove me away. I'll take
what I can get. I am this half-deaf
and wildly nearsighted sun—lowercase—
waiting to rise. Having embraced the aftermath
of my murky fumbling, I am not the clouds.
Then, I'm awake.
               One small sun.

Photograph by Rose Lefebvre

PAULANN PETERSEN, Oregon Poet Laureate Emerita, has six previous full-length books of poetry. Her poems have appeared in many journals and anthologies, including *Poetry*, *The New Republic*, *Prairie Schooner*, *Notre Dame Review*, *Wilderness Magazine*, and the internet's *Poetry Daily*. The Latvian composer Eriks Esenvalds chose a poem from her book *The Voluptuary* as the lyric for a new choral composition that's now part of the repertoire of the Choir at Trinity College, Cambridge. She was a Stegner Fellow at Stanford University, and the recipient of the 2006 Holbrook Award from Oregon Literary Arts. In 2013 she received Willamette Writers' Distinguished Northwest Writer Award.

salmonpoetry

Cliffs of Moher, County Clare, Ireland

"Like the sea-run Steelhead salmon that
thrashes upstream to its spawning ground,
then instead of dying, returns to the sea –
Salmon Poetry Press brings precious cargo
to both Ireland and America in the poetry it
publishes, then carries that select work to its
readership against incalculable odds."

TESS GALLAGHER

The Salmon Bookshop & Literary Centre

Ennistymon, County Clare, Ireland

"Another wonderful Clare outlet."
The Irish Times, 35 Best Independent Bookshops